Let's Have an Adventure

Fair

By Julia Jaske

 I see rides at the fair.

I see tickets at the fair.

 I see popcorn at the fair.

I see lights at the fair.

I see animals at the fair.

I see food at the fair.

I see tractors at the fair.

I see games at the fair.

I see prizes at the fair.

I see carousels at the fair.

I see balloons at the fair.

I see flags at the fair.

Word List

fair	tractors
rides	games
tickets	prizes
popcorn	carousels
lights	balloons
animals	flags
food	

72 Words

I see rides at the fair.

I see tickets at the fair.

I see popcorn at the fair.

I see lights at the fair.

I see animals at the fair.

I see food at the fair.

I see tractors at the fair.

I see games at the fair.

I see prizes at the fair.

I see carousels at the fair.

I see balloons at the fair.

I see flags at the fair.

CHERRY BLOSSOM PRESS

Published in the United States of America by Cherry Lake Publishing Group
Ann Arbor, Michigan
www.cherrylakepublishing.com

Book Designer: Melinda Millward

Photo Credits: Cover: © CGN089/Shutterstock; page 1: © Laura Beach/Shutterstock; page 2: © ThomasPhoto/Shutterstock; page 3: © Misunseo/Shutterstock; page 4: © Janthiwa Sutthiboriban/Shutterstock; page 5: © FooTToo/Shutterstock; page 6: © OmMishra/Shutterstock; page 7: © LMPark Photos/Shutterstock; page 8: © Ganka Trendafilova/Shutterstock; page 9: © Skyler Sargent/Shutterstock; page 10: © Lori Butcher/Shutterstock; page 11: © Curioso.Photography/Shutterstock; page 12: © CreativeMedia.org.uk/Shutterstock; page 13: © Inna Giliarova/Shutterstock; page 14: © SizeSquares/Shutterstock

Cherry Blossom Press is an imprint of Cherry Lake Publishing Group.

Library of Congress Cataloging-in-Publication Data

Names: Jaske, Julia, author.
Title: Fair / Julia Jaske.
Description: Ann Arbor, Michigan : Cherry Lake Publishing, [2023]. | Series: Let's have an adventure | Audience: Grades 2-3. | Summary: "Time for an adventure! Meet us at the fair! Do you know what you'll see while you're there? Books in the Let's Have an Adventure series use the Whole Language approach to literacy, combining sight words and repetition to build recognition and confidence. Keeping the text simple makes reading through these books easy and fun. Bold, colorful photographs that align directly with the text help readers with comprehension throughout the book"—Provided by publisher.
Identifiers: LCCN 2022038128 | ISBN 9781668919101 (paperback) | ISBN 9781668922781 (pdf) | ISBN 9781668921456 (ebook)
Subjects: LCSH: Agricultural exhibitions—Juvenile fiction. | Fairs—Juvenile fiction. | Vocabulary. | Readers (Primary) | CYAC: Agricultural exhibitions—Fiction. | Fairs—Fiction. | Vocabulary. | LCGFT: Readers (Publications)
Classification: LCC PE1119.2 .J37 2023 | DDC 428.6/2—dc23/eng/20220919
LC record available at https://lccn.loc.gov/2022038128

Cherry Lake Publishing Group would like to acknowledge the work of the Partnership for 21st Century Learning, a Network of Battelle for Kids. Please visit http://www.battelleforkids.org/networks/p21 for more information.

Printed in the United States of America
Corporate Graphics